Count Your Way through

Egypt

by Jim Haskins and Kathleen Benson

illustrations by Sue Ramá

M Millbrook Press / Minneapolis

To Jerrell Moore Jr. and Jalyn Moore,

Maeghan Gillon and Myeshia Gillon –K. B.

To teachers of peace, with my gratitude –S. R.

Text copyright © 2007 by Jim Haskins and Kathleen Benson
Illustrations copyright © 2007 by Millbrook Press, Inc.

Millbrook Press, Inc.
A division of Lerner Publishing Group
241 First Avenue North
Minneapolis, Minnesota 55401 U.S.A.

Website address: www.lernerbooks.com

Library of Congress Cataloging-in-Publication Data

Haskins, James, 1941–
    Count your way through Egypt / by Jim Haskins and Kathleen
Benson ; illustrations by Sue Ramá.
      p.   cm. — (Count your way)
    ISBN-13: 978–1–57505–882–5 (lib. bdg. : alk. paper)
    ISBN-10: 1–57505–882–0 (lib. bdg. : alk. paper)
    1. Egypt—Juvenile literature.   2. Swahili language—
Numerals—Juvenile   literature.   3.   Counting—Juvenile
literature. I. Benson, Kathleen. II. Ramá, Sue, ill. III. Title.
DT49.H28 2007
962—dc22   2005033165

Manufactured in the United States of America
1 2 3 4 5 6 – DP – 12 11 10 09 08 07

Introduction

Egypt is located in the northeast corner of the continent of Africa. It borders the Mediterranean Sea on the north, Sudan on the south, and Libya on the west. The Red Sea and the country of Israel lie to the east. Egypt has an area of 386,660 square miles. This is about the same area as the states of Texas and California added together.

The country's official name is the Arab Republic of Egypt. Most of Egypt's 74 million people speak Arabic. The written form of Arabic is very old. It looks something like cursive writing. People read Arabic writing from right to left.

1 ١ (WA-hid)

Egypt has **one** great canal. It's called the Suez Canal.
Boats use the canal to go between the Red Sea and
the Mediterranean Sea. It is the world's longest canal
with no locks. Locks are divisions in a canal. The
Suez Canal was built almost 150 years ago. At first,
Great Britain and France controlled the canal. But
Egypt's government took control of the canal in 1956.

2 ٢ (it-NAN)

The Nile River cuts Egypt into **two** parts.
Deserts lie on each side of the Nile. They are
called the Eastern and Western deserts. The
Nile is the longest river in the world. It flows
through eastern Egypt from the south to the
north. The first Egyptians settled close to the
Nile. Early Egyptians thought of their land as
being divided into the "black land" and the
"red land." The black land was the fertile soil
near the Nile. The red land was the desert that
surrounded the Nile Valley.

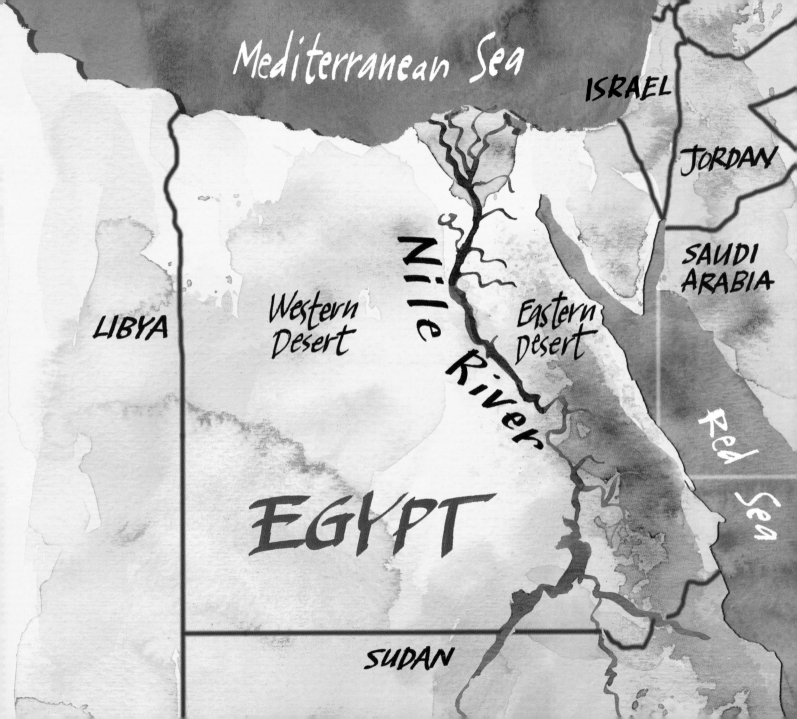

3 ٣ (tah-LAH-tah)

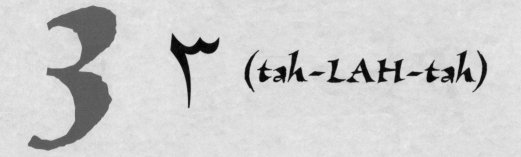

The Egyptian flag has **three** stripes. The red stripe on the top stands for Egypt's struggle for independence. The white stripe is for the revolution that ended the time of Egypt's kings. The black stripe stands for the end of the hard times that the people suffered under the old government. A golden eagle is in the middle of the white stripe. The eagle's feet hold a scroll with the name of the country written in Arabic.

4 ٤ (ar-BAH-ah)

A pyramid has **four** sides. Ancient Egyptians built pyramids as tombs for their kings and queens. Many tourists visit Egypt's pyramids. The most famous is the Great Pyramid in Giza. It stands near the capital city of Cairo. The ancient Egyptians used more than two million stone blocks to build the Great Pyramid. Each block weighed about two tons. That's as much as a car!

5 0 (KAHM-suh)

Most Egyptians eat **five** small meals a day.
For breakfast, they may eat a bean stew
called *ful*. They may eat balls of ground
beans called falafels while going to work or
school. Lunch is usually the largest meal of
the day. Egyptians often eat chicken or beef
with rice and vegetables. After school or work,
they may have a snack of sweet pastries called
baklava or halva. The evening meal often
includes leftovers from lunch or a lamb stew.

Ful

Falafels

Chicken and Rice

Lamb Stew

Baklava

6 7 (SIH-tuh)

These **six** symbols were part of ancient Egypt's writing system. They are called hieroglyphs and make up a kind of alphabet. No one knew how to read the hieroglyphs for hundreds of years. Then soldiers in an Egyptian town named Rosetta found a stone that had both Egyptian and Greek writing on it. Scientists used the Rosetta stone to learn how to read the hieroglyphs.

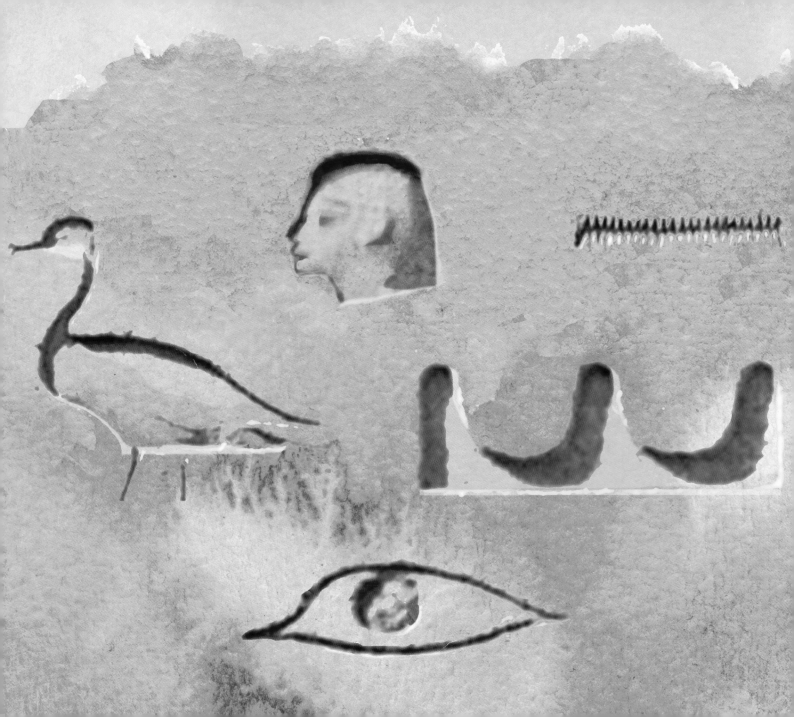

7 ٧ (sah-BAH)

Seven minarets stand over this Egyptian city. Minarets are tall towers that are part of mosques. Mosques are places of worship. Most Egyptians practice the religion of Islam. People called muezzins call out from the tops of these minarets. They remind people to pray. Members of the Islamic faith believe they should pray at least five times a day.

8 ٨ (tah-MAN-yah)

Eight items you might find in an ancient Egyptian tomb are statues, vases, masks, chests, jewelry, paintings, a chair, and a sarcophagus. A sarcophagus is the box that holds a mummy. Ancient Egyptians believed people could take favorite items with them after they died. Dozens of tombs can be found in a place called the Valley of the Kings in eastern Egypt. Famous pharaohs such as King Tut and Ramses III were buried there.

9 (ti-SUH)

Nine products that Egypt sells to other countries are wheat, rice, corn, iron ore, gas, coal, oil, sugar, and cotton. Farmers grow the crops near the Nile River. The soil is good, and the crops can easily be watered. The other products come mainly from the desert. Miners pump for oil and gas that is deep beneath the earth's surface. They dig for coal and iron ore. Egypt also has many modern industries.

Oil

Wheat

Rice

Corn

Sugar

Cotton

Coal

Gas

Iron Ore

10 ١٠ (AH-shah-rah)

Sand Boa

Ten animals that live in Egypt are sand boas, crocodiles, camels, ibises, mongooses, vultures, caracals, desert foxes, sand cats, and scorpions. Many of the country's animals need special survival skills to live in the desert. Animals who don't have these skills stay near the Nile. Food and water are easier to find there.

Scorpion

Sand Cat

Desert Fox

Crocodile

Camel

Ibis

Mongoose

Caracal

Vulture

Pronunciation Guide

1 / ١ / WA-hid

2 / ٢ / it-NAN

3 / ٣ / tah-LAH-tah

4 / ٤ / ar-BAH-ah

5 / ٥ / KAHM-suh

6 / ٦ / SIH-tuh

7 / ٧ / sah-BAH

8 / ٨ / tah-MAN-yah

9 / ٩ / ti-SUH

10 / ١٠ / AH-shah-rah